Pun Dem

PUNDEMONIAM!

the collected puns of

ALAN LEWIS
'The World's Greatest Punster'

with a foreword by

GYLES
BRANDRETH, MP

and illustrated by

'QUANDA'

PAUL WATKINS
STAMFORD
1 9 9 2

Published by
Paul Watkins
18 Adelaide Street
Stamford
Lincolnshire
PE9 2EN

ISBN
1 871615 24 0

Typeset from the disc of the author by
Paul Watkins (Publishing)

Printed and bound by
Woolnoughs of Irthlingborough

CONTENTS

FOREWORD

Just as there are good jokes and bad jokes, so there are good puns and bad puns. This book is a collection of good ones, gems unearthed by AFGL — to give the author his original *Sunday Times* bylined initials — from our marvellous language and deftly cut, polished and displayed for us all to enjoy.

For me the collection proves beyond doubt that those speakers who insist on asking us to pardon the pun either don't appreciate the myriad possibilities and nuances that wordplay has to give or, more likely, are offering us second-rate puns. For, if the pun is something which needs an apology, why did Shakespeare make so much of the genre? Or Dr Johnson, Charles Lamb and Swift?

As a paronomasiac myself, I have to admit that my admiration of AFGL is occasionally tinged with a wisp of envy and frustration that I hadn't thought of a particular twist first. For, like inventions, the best wordplay has an air of the obvious about it, a familiar and comfortable inevitability which belie the effort involved. Some of Alan's work has in fact already passed into the popular subconscious, reappearing from time to time in collections of graffiti and jokes over the past twenty years.

However, oral or aural, visible or risible, I hope you will relish dipping into this pôt-pourri as much as I have. But remember that enjoying such a pôt-pourri will also demonstrate your catholic taste.

To avoid wasting any more of your valuable reading time — at least of the one in seven of you who actually read introductions — I shall leave you with an adaptation of one of the author's own pieces: Alan Lewis is someone who needs no introduction; he is beyond compère.

AUTHOR'S INTRODUCTION

It was in 1971 that I chanced upon the Look Pages of *The Sunday Times* and in particular the punny column-fillers that had been introduced not long before. To my convoluted mind, they were irresistible and I just had to try my hand, even though I had no idea whether the items were commissioned or whether — as I later discovered — they were a national free-for-all. Luck was on my side and, on 30 May, my first pun appeared in print: *Telling bulls from cows is easy; If it's not one thing it's the udder.*

Intoxicated by my success, I turned to punning as a hobby but, like all things worthwhile, found it harder work than I'd imagined. Only rarely was inspiration that obliging and the weekly half-a-dozen submissions were the result of several hours spent with dictionary and thesaurus. Gradually, however, I became more adept and attuned until, after a year or two, I was among the most regularly published contributors. Very occasionally, my efforts were rewarded with more than one piece published on the same day. However, taste is unpredictable and the paper did not always use what I considered my best creations. Each success hid nine rejections. So I decided the solution to the accumulating pile of wordplay was a self-published calendar *Weakly through 1973.*

Just as everything was committed, however, the editor of the Look Pages changed and the new incumbent swept the puns from the page. As a result, the venture lost money and my dream of making a living as a publisher of calendars began to fade rapidly. Encouraged by friends, I nevertheless did go ahead with *Weakly through 1974* which promptly sold out in five weeks and led to calendars for 1975 and 1976. To anyone who's never tried it, I would say that self-publishing is a perilous but emotionally-rewarding pastime. Never will I forget those hectic few weeks of cottage industry mail order each Christmas.

The following year saw an even riskier venture. Not just an arm but a leg was chanced with *A Pun My Soul.* The gamble worked and, with the active support of fans such as John Dunn of BBC Radio 2, the book sold slowly but steadily. In six months, costs were covered and I began to enjoy being a publisher.

Now, more than twenty years since I began writing these pieces, here I am in print again. For me, the big change is that I am no longer the publisher: this time I have to thank Shaun Tyas of Paul Watkins Publishing for having faith in the book's potential.

Pundemoniam includes some pieces that have previously appeared in *The Sunday Times* as well as a few from my own publications. Every one is, as far as I am aware, original. Any apparent plagiarism is totally accidental and unintentional: creative minds sometimes do think alike.

Re-reading some of the older puns has been a strange experience for me but one that reinforces my view that writing them was a process of unearthing rather than invention. I hope you enjoy the discovery as much as I.

Finally, I should like to thank Gyles Brandreth for his kindness over the years. My surprise on first reading his 'world's greatest punster' epithet (in his *Wordplay*) was far greater than Keats's astonishment on first looking into Chapman's Homer!

Alan Lewis,
Naphill,
Bucks.

DEDICATION

For my wife

If you believe in phrenology
You need your head examined

1: CONFUSION, HE SAY

Isn't it odd
That people who are blunt
Soon come to the point?

You can't expect
Christianity
To be totally original
When it began with a crib

Why are they called
Tax Returns
When it
Never
Does?

Do five fish fingers
Make a dab hand?

Printing lies is dangerous
It's libel to hurt someone

A terrorist believes
He has a right
To live and bereave

Is a grass widow
Love lawn?

Most pop fans
Are star-craving mad

Is a singing belly-dancer
Waist recitalling?

Is chiropractic
A wrest cure?

Is someone
Who needs no introduction
Beyond compère?

Is an old flame
Someone you once
Went out with?

Smoking
Is the hot tip
That's a dead cert

Is a tidy drinker
Someone who likes it neat?

Don't put too many adaptors
Into one socket.
They confuse

Are garage mechanics
Keen to maintain differentials?

Billposters are never sacked.
They hand in their notices.

Auction room signalling
Is a nod system

Are firemen awarded
Extinguished service medals?

Is an unspeakable profanity
Ineffable?

Is humble pie
Appease pudding?

11

To refuse a cigarette
Just say
No tar

Is acquiescence
The water of human kindness?

Milk will always stop a watch.
It's the lack tick effect

Are paste diamonds
Carbon copies?

Is hermaphroditism
An end in itself?

Is a gay spark
Free and d.c.?

Back-seat driving
Is a form of duel control

Though I gender up
She keeps asking for more.
I think she must be
An info maniac

Painting the town red
Is easy with a
Roller

When the conductor omitted
The slow movement of my
symphony
I was cut to the quick

At the restaurant
I changed South Korean money
Into Kuwaiti
So it was Dinar for Won

Not many people know
That ignorance is widespread

Do they keep small antiquities
In a morseleum?

Boldness is all about face
Timidity is about face

The essence of voyeurism
Is piquancy

Auction rooms are forbidding

Castles in the air
Are seldom for keeps

13

I met her in the Spring
But lost her on the rebound

2: TRYING FOR SIGHS

Marriage is for better or worse
But these days seldom for good

Their marriage is on the rocks
But things may improve
When they get a bed

She was a gas
But I turned her down.
Now she's an old flame

INFLATUATION
My heart used to pound
When I saw her
But now it only does
A bob or two

She said I had too much
Of the old Adam
And then gave me
The old eve-ho

I fell in love with Dot
But she dashed my hopes
Morse the pity

For lovers
Absence is taxing.
Sort of
Pay as you yearn

I know she thinks
I'm the bee's knees:
She keeps calling me Honey

A lover is like a traitor:
You can expect to be
Turned on by either

Every time I
Sear
I want to be
Wither

When she said 'Howdah do
Take a pew
You look divan'
I thought 'This is sit'
But I was throne aside
When she decided to settle
For a pouffe
A sort of plinth charming
Who promised to support her
For the rest of her dais.
Next time I'll be more chairy

They say that two lovebirds
Can live as cheaply as one
But yesterday I had the bill
And coo!

She told me he was just
A travelling companion
But I sensed
Arrival

As I held her in my arms
She whispered 'I can't wait
Till you hold me again'
And true to her word
She didn't

DIAMONDS ARE FOREVER
When is adore
Not adore?
When it's agate

15

MONETARISTS' CREED
Ingot
We trust

I saw my old flame
At the end-of-therm dance
But when I cauterize
She flared up
Lit a cigarette
And went out

> *He swept her off her feet*
> *But she realised it was just*
> *   flannel*
> *When he tried to sponge on*
> *   her*
> *For the price of a wring*
> *So she gave him the brush off*
> *And made a clean break*

She said I was
The kind she could go for.
Wish I'd been
The kind she could stay for

> *'All of me!*
> *Why not take all of me?'*
> *I asked, as she moved in.*
> *'No thanks', she replied,*
> *'I just want free quarters.'*

When her German boyfriend
Almost caught us together
She said
'That was Klaus!'

> *I odour*
> *A flavour*
> *So I scent her*
> *Some perfume*
> *From an olfactory*

I took a fancy to her
And taking the bull by the
    horns
I seized the opportunity
To take the floor.
I took my time at first
But then took heart
And asked if I could take her
    home
But she said she didn't like
Kleptomaniacs

> *You know it's*
> *Wheel love*
> *When he buys*
> *Her a tyre*

When she cried on my shoulder
I said 'This is so sodden'

> *She started going out with*
> *   rakes*
> *And fell on hard tines*

Hearing she was a fallen woman
I stood her up

> *Stories that sailors*
> *Are amorous*
> *Should be taken*
> *With a pinch of salt*

She doesn't give a
Fig for me
Though all I want
Is a date

> *In her green tweed*
> *It was lovat first sight*

VALENTINE
RHYME
My heart and I
Call to you
But you're too deaf
To Eros

17

A lady cellist
Just lost her job
Through making her scherzo short

3: BEFORE AND DAFTER

Weather vane or not
He's certainly cocky

> *If capital*
> *Is her Seoul aim*
> *You can bet*
> *She's a Korea girl*

Sarah Wanda Elspet Eve
   Townsend
Was initially sweet
But finally
Hated

> *He called me woodenhead*
> *So I gave him*
> *A piece of my mind.*
> *Now he's got*
> *A chip on his shoulder*

She looked right through me.
Didn't even say hollow.
Wish someone
Would fill me in.

> *SEVEN AGES OF MAN*
> *Oat age*
> *Rote age*
> *Vote age*
> *Gloat age*
> *Bloat age*
> *Goat age*
> *Dotage*

My tax form has two headings:
INCOME OWED US
And
INCOMMODE YOU

Why piccolo profession
Like music
That's full of viol practices
Confirmed lyres
Old fiddles
And bass desires?
For the lute, of course

> ***Winning the pools***
> ***Is mere***
> ***Luck***

He's just ordered
A new custom-built piano.
Could it be
Aggrandisement?

> *She has a flare*
> *For the piano.*
> *You can see by her*
> *Very light touch*

The inventor
  of engraving made a pretty
    penny
  of cardboard made a packet
  of astrology made a fortune
  of brooms made a tidy bit
  of carpets made a pile
  of annular sweets made a mint
  of photocopying made a
    million.

> *He said 'If a cutter*
> *Won't prune roses*
> *It won't prune anything'*
> *So I pointed out that that was*
> *A non secateur*

It's my masochist friend's
Birthday.
I can't afford a present myself
So I'm organising
A whip round

He claims the footprint
Is of the abominable snowman
Yeti's evidence is spoorious

If they asked me what
Shakespeare called the Globe
I'd politely say
A wooden O

The king dissolved Parliament
And then took the solute

The bright spark
Who invented aerosols
Made his name
In canned essence

If I told you
I'd been asked for a pun
To celebrate an anniversary
Would jubilee fit?

My twin brother
Takes all my exams.
He's always been able
To pass for me

His pictures
Are atmospheric.
He paints by nimbus

I thought I was £144
In the red
But my bank manager said
That was a gross
understatement

When my ship comes in
I shall push the boat out.

INFLATION IN THE CITY
The doorman
Is in a jamb.
The bunny girl
Is feeling the pinch.
The fan dancer
Is in a ticklish situation.
The barman
Is in a tight corner.
The professional escort
Is being driven to extremities.
And the drug pusher
Is in a fix.

He claimed to be
A professional electrician
But when he held the live wire
I could see he was an ammeter

A kitchen garden
Is just a plot
To keep a husband at home

Those who work for peanuts
Are always shelling out
And it's those with cashew
Can salt some away

When I dropped my clock
In the weedkiller
It made the tick toxic

I could tell from his
Pot plants
That he was a trug addict

'Is the soup chicken?'
'Aye, but the haggis has guts'

21

The Greeks invented
The deep frieze
But didn't think the idea worth
Parthenon

I'm learning to steal.
A cat burglar is teaching
Miaow

When they tract Octavo down
He was a tome
With only his page for
    company.
Not a chapter give in,
He showed his spine
By putting on a bold face
And said he was bound
To ask for proof
Of his sentence.
But their clause were out
And they script him of his
    cuneiform.
His character thus destroyed
He put a bulletin his magazine
    and fired.
He died without issue.

If the police come round
Asking how I came to a choir
The goods
I will refrain from replying.
I chant say anything
Or pass the canon to psalmody
    else.
Whatever the catch
I won't sing

Who'd believe
That after passing seven
Exams in Common Law
He'd die intestate

He's currently
in a cell
in a state of shock
waiting to be charged
with battery.
He says he conducted himself
    well
and offered no resistance.
He re-fuses all food
and asks 'Wire my in here?
Watt have I done?
It wasn't my volt.'
But he'll have to wait faraday
for the circuit judge.

You'd make a splendid
Art thief.
One miniature there
The next miniature not

When I told him
He must clean off the mould
He said there was no must
    about it

24

The police believe
He either drank poisoned coffee
Or was shot in the shrubbery
So they're searching the grounds

WHEN HUE AND DYE WERE SEVENTEEN

Miss Cindy Brown won a crock of gold on a vermilion to one chance which changed her life violetly pastel recognition. She joined the jet set, mixed with film scarlets, and danced her umber with the cream of society. She married Sir Rhys Morgan MP who taught her to lilac a politician and gave her her first khakis (a Silver Shadow). Her flame spread. People called her a tartan worse. But one day she joined the congregation in the puce and realised how jaded she was. When the lesson was red, her cares blue away. She rose up, rust outside to the green and vowed to orange her life anew. Her buff had been called, it was all fawn nothing and she was black white where she'd begun. But would Cerise let Miss Indigo?...

Once upon a time I used
To mispell
To sometimes split infinitives
To get words of out order
To punctuate,- badly
To confused my tenses
To deem old words wondrous
*   fair*
to ignore capitals
To employ common or garden
*   clichés*
To miss the occasional out
To indulge in tautological
*   repetitive statements*
To exaggerate hundreds of
*   times a day*
And to repeat puns quite by
*   chants.*
But worst of all I used
To forget to finish what I

As the judge was in chambers
He was incommoded by my
    request
And I have to see him
At his convenience.
It's a potty system

Thieves broke into the music
*   shop*
And escaped with goods
To the tune of
A silver dollar

The arch crook
Caught an inflection
Started to go round the bend
Took a turn for the worse
And ended up quite kinky

He's a theatre buff
With a tendency to fawn

When she dropped   a line
        me

      my spirits
To raise

   s inclined to think
  a
I w

  h
S e might not be on the level

So I w
   e
    n
     t straight down to see her

Inn a pub
He suggested that
Buy capital expenditure
Ore prospecting
It would be possible
Four me and three others
Too also make money.
But then he's always making
Stupid prepositions.

I THINK THAT I SHALL
NEVER ...
Yew witch, Hazel
It's plane
I'm sycamore poplar girls
And aspen alder time
On the beech
And pine to cedar day
When I'm maple to say
'Hazel lime yours,
Kumquat may'

He was arrested
For jay walking
Larking about
Robin post offices
And several myna offences.
Now he's doing
Eighteen months bird

RE-COLLECTIONS
A pride of plaice
A flock of mattresses
A herd of old jokes
A clutch of straws
A fleet of foot
A litter of picnickers
A haul of fame
A peal of strippers
A cast of fishermen
A crew of interest
A brood of tea
A s'warm of summer greetings
A s'cool of winter greetings

When the witch said
'Abradacabra'
Nothing happened.
She's a hopeless speller

29

I'll be with you
in two sex, said the
hermaphrodite
in half a tick, said the
vivisectionist
in two shakes, said the
freemason
in half a mho, said the
electrician
in a trice, said the Third Man
in necks to no time, said the
executioner
in a flash, said the magician
in an instant, said the
marketing man
in a twinkling, eye said

If there are plenty more
Pebbles on the beach
Why haven't I had
A shingle offer?

Soupçon
Is French for a small amount
Only morceau

Erminaduke and Marmtrude
Are pen-friends.
They've been exchanging letters
For some time

She would keep
Harping on about tidiness
Blowing her own trumpet
And drumming it into me
That I mustn't fiddle
With my hair.
I think she was instrumental
In our divorce

An operatic reputation
Has to be earned.
It's no one's Bayreuth

Some tie marriage knots
With gold
While others prefer
Platinum

A true adman
Writes the prose
And cons

He called me a pessimist
I don't know what it means
But I bet it's something
Horrible

Each night our furry
Purry cat
Would onomatopoeia

Thank you for my Christmas
presents.
The loofah got my back up
The ties made me hot under
the collar
The shaving cream made me
foam at the mouth
The sunglasses made me see
red
The electric blanket made my
blood boil
And the party hat made me
hit the ceiling

You
Who were a gas
Argon

SLIMMING MOTTO
Here today
And gaunt tomorrow

31

Having brought the house down
He said he didn't know
It was liable to claps
(Which seemed applausible
    storey)

SONG FOR SMALL
    MINORITIES
They expect us to flea
But weevil not be moved
Because their propaganda is
    all lice
And mite is right

The Moses film project
Was abandoned
After they'd seen the rushes

Please excuse
Ym shguoc dna sezeens
But I've got this
Terrible code

When the
    psychiatrist
        asked me to
            outline my
                obsessions
            I told him
        I had none
    so I can't
see why he
went on
and on
about
snakes
can
you?

She tried to make me
Take up smoking
But I said
I'd see her inhale first

He's highly strung
And describes himself
As self-taut.
(I think the spelling
Is intensional)

People who're naturally slim
Are usually
Sylph-complacent

My singing teacher says I need a
    tonic
My snooker friends advise a
    break
The drug pusher suggested I take
    a trip
My tailor says I could do with a
    change
The bookseller recommends I
    turn over a new leaf
The pharmacist insists I take five
My osteopath maintains I need a
    wrest
And the lost-property office says
    I should turn it in.
So I'm taking a holiday
To escape the constant advice

I've had this cough
For exactly seven days.
My doctor says
It's just a wee cold

The reproof of the pudding
Is in the repeating

With a glass of whine
You can have a wail of a time
Till the bawl is over

A maxi skirt
Is fine in a bungalow
But a mini
Is better for stares

A rash seasonal wish:
Happy
Eczemas

The fish-processing factory
Had a vacancy
But I couldn't fillet

When you're looking for old
wine
It's always a cellar's market
But when you're selling cows
It's a byre's market

He's doing much butter
Since he found a whey
Of milking his firm of
expenses
When none have been in curd

FIVE MEN, ONE JOB
Marks out
Jacks up
Pats down
Peters out.
Now they're sending a
Bill

JOB ASSOCIATIONS
I remember
Sue veneers.
Chemists say
Anna lies.
Bulls know
Matt adores.
Sailors understand
Sam pans.

He wanted to packet in
So he was completely frank
And addressed himself to his
    boss
Who stamped the floor
And posted him abroad
To sort himself out

His paper business
    Folded
His brassière business
    Went bust
His direct mail concern
    Was written off
His submarine company
    Went under
And his posters
    Went to the wall

Whatever happened
To paper panties?
Did the bottom
Drop out of the market?

If my fate is in the lap
Of the Gods
Then they're not standing up
For me

33

To win the status race
You need two loos

You can't detect
Your own vanity
But others conceit

Though we're all in hock
Life is rosé
Till we get the sack

Chalet or shanty?
It's a decision he should
Dwell on

Continental quilts
Sound fine
But duvet keep you warm?

A white lie
Is aversion
Of the truth

I asked them for a quotation
For a new wall safe
And they said
St Matthew vi. 19

A spire, my son,
But remember
The flèche is weak

An introspective tattooist
Presumably indulges
In self graffitication

She walks with stile
But a drop of portal
Make her gate
Quite wicket

He has 150 cattle.
He thought there were 147
Till he rounded them up

Be flexible
But never lissom
To lithe

An Alpine hydroelectric
scheme
Presumably produces
Off-peak electricity

We live on a triangular estate.
I think we've got the right angle
But you should see
Some of the squares
On the other two sides

He asked me to state
The weight in grammes
But I didn't know
How many to announce

He's so knowledgeable
About ducks
That he tends
To talk down to people

She often gave me a buzz
At the office during the day
But I found out she was
A fly by night

He hasn't got a vocation
To escapology.
He's only in it
For what he can get out of it

35

Have you a green caddy
In wood or iron
With a handicap
Fore putting tee in?
Course we have, sir

Wrestling with the hairpin
He lost his grip
And a slide seemed inevitable
But he regained control without
    turning a hair.
He's a brilliantine-age driver

> *Last knight*
> *A bishop*
> *Was rooked*
> *By a queen*
> *Selling pawn*
> *In the King's Road*

This modern craze
For big engines and fat tyres
Puzzles me.
What's the greater traction?

> *He rants like an old sea-dog*
> *But his barque*
> *Is worse than his bight*

I put all my savings
On a horse
And now I'm a saddler
But wiser man

> *Daddy*
> *Can be caddy.*
> *What else*
> *Is a par four?*

If British Rail introduce
More no-smoking
    compartments
Will it reduce
Pullmanary complaints?

> *'Oil show you to the beach'*
> *She said slickly.*
> *'Tar,' I replied,*
> *As I thought it only pollute*
> *To tanker*

The old Christmas spirit
Is like artificial holly:
Dead and berried

> *The service to*
> *Bury*
> *Is presumably*
> *Inter*
> *City*

The rigging can be
String
But mast bands should be
Brass

> *I told the solitary pedestrian*
> *He had BO*
> *And he replied*
> *'That's why I wore cologne'*

Baldness
Is a kind of failure.
Wish I'd made the greyed

> *If I didn't believe in you*
> *I'd be leaving you*

He's a fair boxer
His swing
Can make a round a bout

It's true
A flower is worth a thousand words
Said the journalist
When he saw the prices on Mother's Day

SEASONAL TOPICS
Spring board
Summer salt
Autumn attics
Winter green

We like to sip
China tea slowly
But samovar friends prefer
Russian

A Siamese twin
Is someone with a strong
Family Thai

MATERIAL WITNESS
She was often canvassed
But never suede

I use a bank
So if my cache is stolen
It will be
Through no vault of mine

For Christmas he wants
A Russian novel
Or the money to buy one
So I'm sending a Chekhov

He gave up breeding strange
  dogs
And now has acute
  melancholy

Santa Claus
Is never seen out on Boxing
  Day:
That's when he has his sleigh
  in

ON BEING FORTY
Is life really
Four nought
Or is it time
Two score
And XL?

I keep my age pianissimo.
When you get to forte
It's aloud

For our holiday this year
We'll be watching TV.
It'll be all week Anna Ford

She's the kind of lasso
Will ring you
Quoit unexpectedly
And once she's round
You can't halter
Flow of noose

Is a group of trainee
Secret service agents
Aspiring?

Avoid racism:
When friends talk of spades
Don't follow suit

Hallo, Buttons,
Haberdasher soda.
It'll give you zip

Writing these is easy.
You jest
Put pun
To paper

39

Newton's thoughts on gravity
Finally bore fruit

4: GRAFGLITTI

Mascara
Makes her eyes smart

A hard woman assumes
The gentle pay

My foot hasn't gone to sleep
It's just comatose

DR FRANKENSTEIN
MADE SOME CREEP FLESH

Dai is volatile
But evanescent

FLOATING VOTERS
CAN SINK A GOVERNMENT

I dislike you some days
But love unites

CORPORAL PUNISHMENT
SMACKS OF SADISM

To paint windows
First draw the curtains

BLOOD IS THICKER THAN WATER
RELATIVELY SPEAKING

When a liar gets pharyngitis
He loses his vice

Have a smashing day tomorrow:
It's Shatterday

SENTIMENTALISTS REMEMBER
LESS TWEE FORGET

THERE ARE TWO KINDS OF PEOPLE -
MARRIED AND CYNICAL

He's a bit of a quiet fish.
I hear he's a piano tuna

BILL STICKERS
PUT YOUR ADHERE

MY CRAZY BOSS
IS OFFICE HEAD

UFOs
Are a saucer contention

Nothing, but nothing, is worth repeating

41

Informers never retire.
They're put out to grass

ONE MAN'S GOOD SCREW
IS ANOTHER'S INFLATIONARY SPIRAL

He always shines
When he's rebuffed

Conscience is
Ought-to suggestion

Spring is here.
Saprise! Saprise!

Goblin your food
Is bad for your elf

AN INDIAN GROCER
IS PRESUMABLY
A DELHICATESSEN

He promised her the earth
And then did the dirty

Man who bury head in sand
Is facing defeat

When my ship comes in
I shall push the boat out

HM Inspector of Taxes
Is an income poop

Etiquette
Tells you how to peel apples.
Decorum
What to do next

Her casserole
Was beyond bayleaf

Is there any Evelyn Waugh?
Pacifists think so!

Nights are getting shorter.
Summaries coming

Unlike clichés
Proverbs last.
Old saws
Keep their edge

WHEN I'M STONED
I GET A LITTLE BOULDER

Police cuts
Mean fewer nicks

TYPEWRITER CORRECTION FLUID
IS THE MEANS TO AMEND

Youth is
prime pasture.
Middle age is
pasture prime

A.I.D.
Isn't exact
It's a
Proxy mate

All zoos aren't pointless.
In ours
The tapir's at one end

5: SUTURE SELF

They say he's toffee-nosed
But I think
A lot of it's humbug

The newspaper's story
On the half man, half horse
creature
Was in the centaur spread

The palmist told me I'd be
(a) moral
(b) knighted
(c) cured and
(d) graded
But I didn't understand
Her next point about being
Jected

TV CRITIC
When the puff on the box
Says it's a bran-new cereal
I always know it'll be
The same old corn

There was a little girl
Who had a little curl
Right in the middle of her
forehead
When she was good
She was very very good
But when she was bad ...
(See next edition for Part 2
of this quiff-hanger)

Don't worry
About my grammar
She's parsed it.

I tolerated my wife's
Ideas on women's lib
Till she suggested role-
swapping
Then I put her foot down

I was in two minds whether
to stay
But my wife had half a mind
to go
So we went

It isn't the confetti
That gives newlyweds away
But the rice to the bedroom

He claims that his
'What the butler saw' machines
Are art dekko

In Hollywood's early days
They took a role
And made De Mille of it

We nicknamed the club's
bouncer
Zeus
Because he can handle
Titans

With a knees-up
You're sure to get
A shindig

He says he has
Gold fever
But it's fluorite

45

My doctor discovered
I was afraid of going west.
He calls it Gloucesterphobia

The wealth of doctors
Lies in coffers

Noise can cause headaches.
In fact nothing acts faster
Than a din

I was going to pieces
Till the doctor told me
Not to excerpt myself

He likes
Mammoth meat sandwiches
With mastodon

We call our cat
Peapod
Because he's got
Mange too

I've been going
Backwards and forwards
To the doctor for treatment
And am half cured.
Now I only go forwards

Her enthusiasm
For coffee icing
Puts the moccas on her baking

My insurers offered 75%
For the damage
As they claim to treat all floods
As freak waters

I've just been on a cookery
course
In central France.
I never saw the Auvergne
cleaner

MOTTO FOR STARRY-
EYED DIETERS
If you want a heavenly body
Planet

I tried to develop
A recipe for hyena soup
And ended up
Making myself a laughing stock

If my boss
Blotted his copybook
No one would dare blame
His nibs

I knew he'd been stealing
My glass bottle designs
When I went through his phials

My neighbour asked
If I would introduce his son
To my window-cleaning
business
So I took the ladder round

The chick-pea starter was
poisoned
He said, posthoumously

If a goalie
Is fond of the odd foul
Is he a paltry keeper?

The new dentist said he was
Just filling in
And gave me
A locum anaesthetic

KEEN PHILOSOPHER'S
MOTTO
'Ave id
Will travel

He tried to walk on water
In one of his lighter moments

I hear you solved
The eternal triangle
By using geometry.
Here's looking at Euclid!

SCIENTIST'S MOTTO
However fine doubt
Find out

In O-level maths
We had to divide 22 by 7.
It was easy as pi

French leave
Is when people depart
Without further adieu

I've invented a sonic telescope
So that even when it's dark
I can get a peep out of it

He was covered from head to
foot
In bits of man-made fibre.
I'd never seen him
In such acetate

Every judo suit
Should be sold with a needle
and cotton
So one is ready for the fray

Because I upset my tailor
He gave me
A cuff round the ear

I bought my diary
in an annual sale
My feeler gauges
in a clearance sale
My chest-expanders
in a spring sale
(or was it a redevelopment
sale?)
My hormone rooting powder
in a stocktaking sale
And my clock
in a winding-up sale

At the Oval
I had a Nova
From the Vauxhall end

TENNIS MOTTO
Badger the umpire.
He'll give you the set

Ma, the robot is
Mechanize at me!

He says he drives
At a snail's pace
But you should see escargot

Nothing's perfect.
Even team spirit
Has side effects

The reason I doubt the claims
Of second-hand car salesmen
Is missed rust

Even if pigs could fly
They'd probably
Go into a stall

49

Evel Knievel
Was refused entry
To our local cinema
After he'd jumped the queue

6: CORES AND DEFECT

I lost the hiccuping competition
Because someone gave me a start

In a traffic hold-up
My speech gets fruity
Because the jam jars

He put his flannel shirt
On a horse
Because it was napped

Because the other boxer
Was wiping the floor with him
His seconds threw in the towel

He's calling his new bookshop
'The One Plus One'
Because it specialises
In first additions

They call her a slat
Because she's anyone's
Louvre

If you iron ox-hide
It could go a rusty colour

My son says when he grows up
He'll be a mathematician,
a carpenter, or a waiter
Because his teacher told him
He's good at tables

ASSAY! ASSAY!! ASSAY!!!
Why is eternity trying?
I don't know:
Why is eternity trying?
Because it's for ever
Endeavour

The Three Wise Men
Each carried only one gift
Because they had believed
In travelling light

He wears a tweed deerstalker
Because he believes
It's the right tec style

A lady estimator
Has just been given
A bit of a roasting
Because they wanted her
tender quickly

My boss said
I should be fired with
enthusiasm
And because I wasn't
I was

Danny la Rue would make
A good St George in panto
Because he's used to coping
With the drag on

I invented a boy jelly-baby
But it didn't sell well
Because the novelty
Soon wore off

51

Because he bolts
His food
He keeps getting fetter

If a man asks a woman
To help him with a crowbar
It's because
He can't lever alone

I knew someone
Had used my saw for a lark
Because the edge
Was a little burred

I know he had
An old-fashioned name
Because yclept it secret

I knew it was Miss Muffet
On the tuffet
Because she had
A whey with her

Because she believed in
Petticoat rule
I gave her the slip

Because I'm going bald
I'm a bit tonsure of myself
And if anyone mentions it
There's hell toupee

Only a husband
May call his wife
A baggage
Because she's a special case

I don't understand American
slang.
On tv last night
They called a guy a sucker
Because he blew it!

METRICULATION

As I 2.54centimetred my way along the ledge, I could feel my heart 0.454kilogramming with the fear that I might fall like a 6.35kilogrammes to the 0.914metres below. I paused a 12.7kilogrammes of the way along with one 30.5centimetres 5.03metred precariously on a short 5.03metres projecting from the wall.

0.142litres would be a 1.61kilometres away by now but anyway I had no 1.29grammes about her, as I'd had that 4.55litres my mind for far too long.

I summoned every 28.2grammes of strength, grasped a rusty 20.1metres with both 10.2centimetres and slid to the ground. I could hear a hen nearby 9.10litring at some loose 0.0648grammes. Once down, I tried to 1.83metres why our plan had misfired, what was the 20.1centimetres I had overlooked, the 1859 metres/hour I had yet to untie?

See key on page 88.

I do envy artists.
I'd give my right ear
To be able to paint
Like Van Gogh

7: IDLE THWARTS

When will we learn
That knuckle down
Doesn't mean
Hold out your hand

Whether there really is
A silent majority
Is a mute point

I'm completely in the dark
About labour relations.
Is blacking
The same as going sloe?

I was young
Once.
Wish it had been
Twice

Old age is when
Your heir apparent
Becomes a parent

LITERARY PUN
The race is not always to the
Swift
Means you can't
Houyhnhnm all

Prices are rising faster
Than my salary.
Things are getting disparate

I try to make
The pound go further
But I can't
Budget

Our college offers:
A sandwich course in catering
A day release course on
    probation
And a crèche course in baby
    minding

I told her no sensible man
Would take her dancing
In her bikini
So she went
With a little moron

If English printers
Sing in quires
Do French ones
Sing in reams?

I long for a world
Where ignorance is unknown
Silence unheard of
And archaeology a thing of the
    past

The thing that puzzled
    Newton
Was how it was an apple
Could fall
When it had been plum
Overhead

D-DAY IN MEMORIAM
Fond thoughts of Bob
Last seen 14 February 1971
From your ever-changing
Penny

ADVICE TO THIEVES
Wear a stocking mask.
Denier won't be recognised

A barrister is someone
Who can turn a plain tiff
Into a fancy argument

If you run out
Of pain-killers
I have some morphia

I'm publishing a book
On incentives for security
men
Called 'The good guard goad
guide'

He does an excellent pastiche
Of a science fiction writer.
Asimov to a T

Crosswords are infuriating
They're always putting
1 across
Which tends to get 1 down

'George Bernard Shore was born
in Island'
Is both a littoral mistake
And a printer's Eire

I proposed as the radio played
The bridal march
From Lohengrin.
It seemed like
An opera tune movement

Memorable babysitters
Are readily called to mind

The Keating painting
Seemed vaguely familiar.
Sort of Degas vu

The strip show
Was disappointing
But luckily
There was no redress

'You've waltzed with me
enough'
Said my dancing teacher.
'Now it's time
You stood on your own feet'

MONEY TO BURN
Rockets are 50p upwards
Catherine wheels are around 75p
Bangers are a shattering 20p
Sparklers are pretty pricey
And Roman Candles are still
shooting up

I've just seen a stage version
Of the Female Eunuch.
The cast rating was excellent

The record shop
Had two versions
Of Ravel's *Bolero*
But I didn't like the sleeves

As long as
I can rely on tranquillisers
I haven't given up opiate

Craftiness
Is not easily acquired.
It takes a wile or two

A diet of Frankenstein
Always puts me to sleep.
Sort of sop horrific

Because she said
'You get up my nose'
I knew
I adenoid her

He looks rather more than
Wan.
I think his trouble may be
Pleural

Is the measure
Of a lean time
How much people tip?

At night I lay awake
Wondering what I'd do
If ever I suffered from
Insomnia

When I'd had a jar
I said 'Ewer
As pretty as a pitcher'
But now I'm on the wagon
I'm surrey
I opened my trap

EASTER DIET
Ovoid
Chocolate

Schnapps
And hock
Are my favourite
Teutonics

If bar drinks go metric
I hope it's
Schooner rather than litre

A tied pub
Is presumably
A trussed house

If you disagree
With the dentist's decision
Don't remain silent:
Have it out

BUSINESS MOTTO
The less pull you have
The more push you'll need

If you perpetually
Bow and scrape
You'll always be second fiddle

Those who offer
To carry the can
Are often given
The sack

He tried to put my mind at rest
But I was using it all the time

Putting things
In a nutshell
Often reveals
A kernel of truth

To regard the world
As your oyster
Has always seemed to me
A little shellfish

I feel so strongly
About loo graffiti
That I've signed
A partition

58

The suit he offered me
Was too loud
So I turned it down

Thank God
I'm an atheist
Touch wood
I'm not superstitious
And I never
Damn well swear

In a quarrel at Wimbledon
I played both ends
To the middle
And got the centre caught

If a huge weight of rock
Can produce diamonds
Would half the weight
Lead to semi-pressures stones?

Suits described as
Out of this world
On me look like
Nothing on earth

I'm learning about horses' tack
Bit by bit

I hate friction
So I tend
To let things slide

I told my boss
What I really thought of him
And in return
He put my cards on the table

They told me . . .
He'd gone west
He'd gone for a Burton
He'd kicked the bucket
He'd fallen asleep
He'd gone over
He'd pegged out
He'd given up the ghost
He'd died

So I assumed . . .
It was occidental death
He'd had a fit
He'd been impaled
He'd taken an overdoze
He was a brain defect
He'd been intent on dying
He'd taken too much exorcize
He was a theatrical failure

60

8: PACKAGED EELS

He's a sage old salt
Keen as mustard
Whose life has been peppered
By capers in Chile.
He calls himself
A seasoned professional.

Her millinery is old hat
Her carriages are hackneyed
Her picture frames are passé
Her walnut loaf is dated
And her broom handle is stale

He's always
Elbowing his way in
Which makes him look
High-handed

At school
My son had an A for effort
And an E for achievement
Which is why he failed
Spelling

They've changed
The sandwich course in Spanish
To a pancake course
And put up a notice saying
'Spanish tortilla'

When they saw
A nut
Bolt
During prison drill
They studied his file
And nailed
A screw

After the music examiner
Had played a short piece
He asked me to state the time
And to beat it
So I said 'Half past ten'
And left

My late aunt left a strange will:
The booby trap's mine
And the ship yaws.
The bier's hearse
And the snake's hiss.
The time-scale is hours
And theirs the rub.

When I went to the bank
About my loan
The manager pointed to the
*   door*
And said it was foreclosing

Education should always be
Comprehensive
Though the
Technical
Should never be
Secondary
To the
Grammar

As he sat there
With knitted brows
The odd serge of emotion
Heart felt sympathy
And a little flannel
I could tell he was
A man of the cloth

61

She avoids bare-faced lies
By adopting false hoods

I had a little beef
In the butcher's
And a grouse
In the poulterer's.
My wife says
I complain too much

I've suggested he becomes
A swimming instructor
Or an artist
Or takes up rowing
But he refuses to do a stroke

If they brought back
Duelling
Would it make
A scrap of difference?

I knew the 8 o'clock train
Was ahead of schedule
Because it left
About twenty to wait

Her toy guardsman's arm
Had broken off, so I
Sold her soldier shoulder solder

She's mad about reptiles:
Studying them is her pet ology.
Whereas I took an exam in
*   fungi:*
It was my set ology

When your car battery is flat
It doesn't matter whether
Your knight has shining armour
Just as long as he has
His charger with him

I was going to be a vegetarian
Until I discovered
Potatoes have eyes
Wheat has ears
Cabbages have heads
Some beans are kidneys
And artichokes have hearts

The Oxford and Cambridge
    boat race
Involves two prime eights
Trying to make monkeys of
    each other

One man said I was yellow
Another said I looked blue.
So I've joined the Green party

A dictator is someone
Who doesn't let
The man in the street
Get in the road

The church disco was a flop.
The record of Genesis
Led to a mass exodus

When we were told
On the camping holiday
To sleep under the stars
It seemed a portent

By putting high pressure on
*   Asia*
The weatherman made it a
*   dry forecast*
And putting low pressure on
*   Europe*
Mediterranean

The hotel porter refused
To carry my baggage
So I punched him.
My case comes up next week

'I'm just a dogsbody'
Can be a cri de cur

Some say he's a bully
But he struck me as a gentle person

9: MORES, FEWER WISE

My aunt
Sedate days
But staid
Longer

The only time
I can move mountains
Is in a fit of pique

A gentleman is someone
Who always offers a lady
Deceit

She says
Her cat talks to her
But it's mews to me

A bigot is someone
Whose train of thought
Runs on narrow gauge

'Right', I said,
'All hands to the plough'
And everyone went to the pub

Tree surgeons
Think a lot of themselves.
They're always taking boughs

They said he was
Small beer
But I reckon he was
Lager than life

She says 'I's way out'
When pretending to be an egress

He's smarmy.
Oozy think he is?

Whatever the colour
Of a country's politics
Its embassies are always
In violet

Politics
Is the art
Of getting your views a cross

You can tell
He's going to seed
By the grain
At the temples

His hobby is collecting
waistcoats.
He only has the one pursuit

I composed a new
National Anthem
But the die-hards said
They wouldn't stand for it

An only son
Was disinherited
When he insisted his parents
Let their heir down

When a lad starts
To shave
He begins to think
Of paring off

If you want to call the tune
You need to know the score
Or you might end up
Playing second fiddle

Is a dunce's hat
The height of stupidity?

He may be
The apple of his mother's eye
But he's a rotten pupil

In the speed-typing
competition
We had to fill a page.
I won by a wide margin

My invention
Of 100 watt stereo headphones
Was an ear disaster

I could tell he was unfamiliar
with French music
By his first Fauré
into conducting

When the examiner asked me
What Armageddon meant
I thought it was the end of the
world

Maid Marion
Already had a bow and arrow
When Robin made her quiver

If your prayer book
Is a small volume
It may have been written
By St Francis half a c.c.

She's one of the illuminati
Since she literati cigarette

He looks a little drained
Since I bailed him out

When I asked him
To put his money
Where his mouth is
He pursed his lips

When people cook their books
Taxmen are likely
To have them for dinner

There's nothing to bricklaying
But mortar pointing

If you're insolvent
You can't even
Dissolve into tears

If you try to touch me
For a loan
You'll be surprised
At the tactile show

I'm still waiting
For my ship to come in
But my neighbour has
A mast enough

I'm making arrangements
To display my flowers
And taking steps
To do more walking

Weed gardening yesterday
Weave embroidery today
Wheel roll up tomorrow

When the animals entered the ark
Two by two
Noah didn't know
Where they'd be making four

I'd like gardening
If I didn't have to
Dig
Sow
Mulch

Five minutes ago
I killed an ant.
Looks as though
Nest of kin have been informed

They go french polishing
On alternate evenings.
It's his turn to stain tonight

When the policeman
Found himself shoplifting
He thought he was dreaming
So he pinched himself

Are all JPs equal?
Or is there a pecking order
For beaks?

After the police arrested
The cat burglar
They found safe-breaking tools
On his persian

The judge refused to
pronounce
A long sentence
Arguing it was beyond
His jury's diction

If the other man's grass
Is always greener
That's sod's law

She was a hothead.
He was a dry old stick.
But they made a good match

Who was it said
That pithy quotations
Are remembered long after
Their authors are forgotten?

Sure of my facts
I said I'd eat my hat.
Many a true word's spoken
Ingest

I find modern literature
Less meaty than of old.
Today a Mark Twain
Would write Tom Soya

He turned up late for the duel
And then shot the second
So they charged him
With killing time

To be tied to someone's apron
strings
Doesn't always mean accord

As the jury have all disappeared
Said the judge
I shall record a verdict of
Clear doubt.

I don't expect to be
In the doghouse for long
So I've only taken
A short leash

When I made my mother-in-law
An offer of a new broom
I didn't expect she would ever
Take me up on it

The campanologist
Was prosecuted by the Noise Abatement Society
And lost on a peal

If your kids
Get your goat
Find a nanny!

When she said
'Come on, dear'
I refused.
I hate being commandeered

My children prefer
punishment
In the heat of the moment
Rather than waiting
Till I scold

Had a few biers
At the Hearse of the Year Show
And couldn't keep a wake
Next mourning

As the vet
Calmly carried the medicine
Into the lion's cage
I could see
He had what it takes

When he applied for the job
Of human cannon-ball
They took him like a shot

Every July
My children solemnly agree
Father Christmas doesn't exist
But by December there's a
Claus in their agreement

I call her Chris Alice
'Cause I larva dearly

Because she's overweight
She diets
Goes to keep-fit classes
Has regular saunas
And employs a masseur.
It's a case of
No expanse spared

When he discovered
A cure for vertigo
His fame soon rose
To dizzy heights

Drink chilled white wine
With bream
And if you have red
Mullet

If you don't want to end up
In the cart
Stay on the wagon

With one over the eight
You'll be at sixes and sevens
And end up on all fours

Snail-eating contests
Are won by those
Who have first prise

After I dropped
The mixture on the floor
The decision had to be
Abort cake

Porous
A drink
And filter
The brim

74

The dentist was caught out
By the paperwork.
He had too many
Indentures

I offered him
One for the road
And he said 'Make it a double -
It's a dual carriageway.'

We'd willingly take
Our wives along
If pubs would serve
Better halves

Keep getting your wires
    crossed
And you'll end up with a mesh

I used to be
A touch typist
Till one slapped my face

He was a loafer
Till he went on a sandwich
    course.
Now he's the breadwinner

To cope now and then
With the ins and outs
Of the comings and goings
And ups and downs
He's found a new approach
That's quite a departure

The trouble with
Making a pretty penny
Is that you can be
Arrested for counterfeiting

I threatened
To strike a bargain
But before I could
He knocked me down

He claimed to have
An inclination towards sales
So we asked him to produce
Evidence of bias

A dark horse
Should be avoided.
You're better off
On your roan

People who indulge
In word play
Certainly get up to
Semantics

PRAYER OF THE
    CONFUSED COBBLER
May my sole
Be heeled

If life seems rosy
It's probably
A pigment of the imagination

When I advertised for a
    secretary
The response was thick and
    fast.
I hope the next applicants
Will be more intelligent and
    shy

Letting welshers
Go scot free
Sounds Irish to me

The trouble with fireballs
Is that they often won't
Put themselves out

THE SNOW MUST GO ON
It'll be all white on the night

If someone says
'Leave everything to me'
Are they
Self-willed?

Pacifism promotes
The thinker not the thong

    Is that a catechumen, son?
    No, it's a dogma

As an extreme Protestant
He's against merging the
    churches.
His motto is
No pot-pourri

    It can be quite a shock
    When a live wire
    Comes down to earth

Why call watches
Digital
When they have no
Fingers?

    My maths master explained
       everything
    In no uncertain terms
    Which is why I failed
    Algebra

We were always at odds
Till I put one over.
Now we're even

    What happened to your cap,
       Stan?
    It blew off in the wind, lass

If he no longer
Turns you on
Perhaps it's time
For a switch

    Choose a sado-masochist.
    She's bound to love you

I'm a bit chicken
Where birds are concerned
But I somehow need less pluck
If she's well dressed

    Their plan to scrap
       shoe-repairers' equipment
    Is a last ditch attempt

A free waxwork of a Mercian
    king
Was an Offa he couldn't refuse

    Though I lost my temper
    And yelled at everyone
    In the motorist's shop
    I couldn't get a solenoid

In the sale
The duvet was marked down
But it turned out to be feather

    People are strange.
    They go to the sales
    For a few seconds
    And spend hours there

Though he worked hard
Teaching me the art of rowing
He never got it into my scull

He believes in corporal punishment
But then he's always been a smart arse

When a referee blows his whistle
Does it make his pulse race?

Is the fellowship
Of photographers
Cameraderie?

The winner
Can never take all
Since others
Have to take part

I invented a macadam
Playing surface for cricket
But the bowlers found the
*   balls*
Tended to be overpitched

I've just won the sweep
And we don't even have
A chimney

She kept nagging
Her sculptor boyfriend
To make some bronze
*   cricketers*
Till he cast her a side

It's her fear of the colour red
In roulette
That makes her bête noire

If you wear
A dog collar
You're expected
To take the lead

Is a yawning chasm so-called
Because people keep dropping
    off?

I hadn't thrown a boomerang
For years
But it soon
Came back to me

He was tickled to death.
The verdict was man's laughter

Strange
But almost every pig in a poke
Is sold by a cowboy

My waist used to be 28 inches
But it's not any longer!

No one interrupted
My fund-raising speech
But everyone chipped in

I thought he'd given me
A reference
But it was just an
Allusion

They buried over half a score
(No pun in ten dead)

What makes her French cooking
Streets ahead?
Why, the rue sauce

When a business
Runs right down
It has to be
Wound up

She spun him
A rather thin yarn
Embroidering as she went along
It was crewel to watch

Critics of America
See Uncle Sam
As an Aunt Sally

10: GROAN UPS

I've just realised
Why your face
Reminds me of a clock:
Your lips tick

I asked our switchboard
  operator
For a line
And she said
'My husband doesn't understand
  me'

No longer has he
Girls upon his knee
Just laps of memory

She'll do anything
For a song and a drink.
So we offered a roundelay

As a bank manager
My only interest
Is to get you a loan
And make advances

I've put my money
Into a new girlie magazine
So I can take
Accrued interest

When Eve offered Adam
The apple
They realised for the first time
They had no cloves

Is the design of French knickers
An open brief?

Wife swappers believe
That marriage is
For barter or worse!

Divorce happens
When the melody of love
Becomes just another strain

Marriage proposals used to be
Question the pop
Then pop the question

I can always tell
When my wife's dreaming
  she's Titania:
She keeps Oberon her side of
  the bed!

Monogamy
Leaves a lot
To be desired

The eternal triangle
Is usually
Right tangled

Courtship
Is when you try each other
For sighs

When she said carrion
I was dead sure
I cadaver

A lot of pillow talk
Is just said
To bolster

82

Brass monkey weather
Is when it's
Minus two

When she said
I could kiss her on the groyne
I knew I was on
A shore thing

Don Juan
Carved nicks in the bedpost
So he could count
The noches

Telling bulls from cows
Is easy.
If it's not one thing
It's the udder

After another woman
Had turned his head
He couldn't face his wife

Do flagellants find
That the switch
Turns them on?

Because she has
A 39.37 inch bust
Men love to metre
But I don't know what they see
In the two decimal places

Her two-timing
Eventually spoilt
Hour
Secs

I can't sleep
When the night wears on
And don't want to
When the nightwear's off

I'll look after my secretary
At the office party
And make sure
She's not wanton for nothing

PERMISSIVE THOUGHT
Love all
is a bit
noughty

SEX LIFE
Nineteen plenty
Twenty-nine flirty
Thirty-nine forte
Forty-nine thrifty
Fifty-nine three score
Sixty-nine eventually

She put her arms around me,
Squeezed and said
'This is my only vice'

She's not little any more
She's a beguile now

She's clearly a verse to him
So how he stanza
I don't know.
Perhaps it's her lovely L-E-G's

Just had a wartime dream.
I was with a squad
Of eighty yes girls

Spanish Fly
Is strong stuff.
You only need
Half a Si Si

He found his wife had a lover
When he caught the fast twain

A capital lover
Writes small letters
But believes in largesse for
Sex

If his new secretary
Isn't sweet in the daytime
And a little tart at night
He'll saccharin the morning

> *When she said*
> *I could make her mine*
> *I knew*
> *She was a gold-digger*

She's the May Queen
I hope to be May King

> *I could tell*
> *From her 41-31-37*
> *measurements*
> *That she was in her primes*

Women say
She dresses like a tart
But she suits
The guise

> *Cosmetic surgery has given*
> *her*
> *An ampoule bosom*

Very well, said Eve,
Take it
Or leaf it

> *The Marx on her neck*
> *Showed she'd had Lenin*

I'm going abroad
For wine, women and song.
The triple do me good

> *Cleopatra always said no.*
> *She was the queen of denial*

My new sex manual
Is all embracing

When she invited him
Into her tent
She hoped the guy
Would stay

> *Weight-lifting*
> *Is a hard way*
> *To hernia living*

His divorce
Was a lass ditch bid
For freedom

> *Whenever I have*
> *A night on the tiles*
> *My wife hits the roof*

When it's a needle match
I like to get my eye in first

> *EEC PUN*
> *My Natasha*
> *Is a German bag*

After the singing teacher
Had put me through the hoop
My voice was croquet

> *The difference between love*
> *and lust*
> *Is that the first is real*
> *And the second just*
> *reproduction*

These days
Living together
is taken as wed

FIN

OTHER HUMOUR TITLES
FROM PAUL WATKINS
(Each of which contains some punny material)

BOOK-WORM DROPPINGS
The hilarious collection of absurd remarks overheard in second-hand bookshops, edited by Shaun Tyas and illustrated with copious cartoons by Martin Smith. The paperback version now in its third impression. Cited in *The Guardian* editorial as an example of a book that would never win a literary prize!
Octavo, 128 pages, £5.95 paperback (ISBN 1 871615 01 1) *or:*
£9.95 500-copies limited edition hardback (ISBN 1 871615 00 3).

MORE BOOK-WORM DROPPINGS
The wonderful sequel, put together by the same team, contains contributions from new bookshops and libraries.
Octavo, 128 pages, £5.95 paperback (ISBN 1 871615 06 2) *or:*
£9.95 500-copies limited edition hardback (ISBN 1 871615 14 3).

THE ILLUSTRATED HISTORY OF THE WORLD
WITH PICTURES!
Created by Professor David Rowe, this satire on tabloid journalism reports history as it might have been told by the tabloids of the day. The newspaper in question is 'The Big Shiny Thing in the Sky' or **The Big S**. Described by *The Times* as 'splendid'.
A4, 96 pages, £5.95 paperback (ISBN 1 871615 18 6) *or:*
£12.95 hardback (ISBN 1 871615 17 8).

Order from your local bookseller or post-free direct from the publisher:

Paul Watkins,
18 Adelaide Street,
Stamford,
Lincolnshire, PE9 2EN
Tel: (0780) 56793.

KEY TO METRICULATION (page 53)
inch pound stone yard quarter foot perch pole gill mile scruple gallon ounce chain hand peck grain fathom link knot.